*Quick*GUIDES

everything you need to know...fast

Working With Volunteers

by Cherry Bushell

reviewed by Jinny Gender

WIREMILL
PUBLISHING LTD

Across the world the organizations and institutions that fundraise to finance their work are referred to in many different ways. They are charities, non-profits or not-for-profit organizations, non-governmental organizations (NGOs), voluntary organizations, academic institutions, agencies, etc. For ease of reading, we have used the term Nonprofit Organization, Organization or NPO as an umbrella term throughout the *Quick*Guide series. We have also used the spellings and punctuation used by the author.

Published by
Wiremill Publishing Ltd.
Edenbridge, Kent TN8 5PS, UK
info@wiremillpublishing.com
www.wiremillpublishing.com
www.quickguidesonline.com

British Library Cataloguing in Publication Data
A catalogue record for this book is available from the British Library.

ISBN Number 1-905053-18-5

Printed by Rhythm Consolidated Berhad, Malaysia
Cover Design by Jennie de Lima and Edward Way
Design by Colin Woodman Design

Disclaimer of Liability
The author, reviewer and publisher shall have neither liability nor responsibility to any person or entity with respect to any loss or damage caused or alleged to be caused directly or indirectly by the information contained in this book. While the book is as accurate as possible, there may be errors, omissions or inaccuracies.

CONTENTS

WORKING WITH VOLUNTEERS

INTRODUCTION

A definition of the word "volunteer" is "to perform or offer to perform a service of one's own free will." This encapsulates most of the issues that arise for volunteers and the nonprofit organisations (NPOs) that use them. Volunteering is a key activity for many NPOs. The decision to involve volunteers for the first time will have a major impact on an NPO, so it is vital to consider all the issues in advance. Having volunteers is not an end in itself.

Volunteers contribute in a variety of ways from behind-the-scenes efforts to high-profile fundraising and awareness-raising. Their contributions can be extremely valuable, so time and effort spent planning will help to ensure their involvement will be worthwhile for both the NPO and themselves.

This Guide will help NPOs be more welcoming and attractive to potential volunteers and avoid problems by planning ahead. It seeks to answer questions such as:

What are our goals and objectives for involving volunteers? What is the purpose of volunteer tasks? What work will volunteers do and not do, and why? What do we expect volunteers to accomplish? How can we make sure we are finding the best ways to put volunteer skills to work? What outcomes do we want volunteers to achieve? How will we evaluate success?

WHY VOLUNTEERS?

WHY DO PEOPLE VOLUNTEER?

People volunteer for a number of reasons. They have time on their hands – they may be retired or between jobs or don't work. They may want to do a job but don't want the commitment of paid work. They may want to learn a new skill. Or most commonly, they want to help your organisation. Although volunteering is freely given, volunteers will have expectations that need to be understood and met.

SHOULD YOU TAKE ON VOLUNTEERS?

Be sure that you have good reasons for taking on volunteers. Not every organisation has or needs volunteers. Having a clear reason why you want volunteers, and knowing what they will do and how you will manage them are crucial to success.

Good reasons to have volunteers can include the following:

- Volunteers can bring to the NPO a wider section of society or the community, clients (those who are the beneficiaries of your services) and other stakeholders (those who have other interests in the organisation).

- Volunteers can enhance the work of the NPO – they extend the capacity of paid staff in terms of numbers, hours and skills.

- Volunteers can be adaptable in terms of what they do, the time they give, and how they cope with changes of tasks and expectations.

- Volunteers can contribute new ideas and a fresh perspective.

- Volunteers can bring specialist skills that would otherwise be too expensive for an organisation.

- Volunteers can concentrate on specific, in-depth or very narrow pieces of work.

- Volunteers can "spread the word" about the NPO in a way that advertising and marketing cannot.

- An NPO that has successful and powerful volunteer involvement is a very attractive one and often receives more respect, credibility and interest on the strength of it.

- Volunteers often become donors as well!

Continues on next page

Negatives should also be taken into account when deciding whether to have a volunteer programme. Issues include:

- Volunteers cost money (recruitment, running a volunteer programme, staffing, etc.).

- Volunteers are not a temporary solution to a paid-staff shortage or gap.

- Volunteers take staff time.

- Jobs shouldn't be made up in order to have volunteers. If you don't need them, don't have them.

- Volunteers need to be taken seriously, and their time should not be wasted.

- Volunteers should not be taken on because funders or other interested parties either suggest it or put pressure on the organisation to do so.

- A volunteer programme should not be instituted because other organisations have one.

Clear and thoughtful evaluation of the pros and cons of having volunteers is crucial before embarking on a volunteer programme.

TYPES OF VOLUNTEER ROLES

Volunteers can fulfil a vast range of roles and functions and the key ones can be divided as follows.

Service Provision

Volunteers can participate in the work in which your organisation engages. This can include:

- Client support

- Befriending

- Drivers

- Trainers

- Helpline operators

- Advisors

Fundraisers

Volunteers can assist in your fundraising activities. They can act as:

- Networkers

- Fundraising committee members

- Collectors

- Event organisers

- Treasurers

- Researchers

WHY VOLUNTEERS?

Administration
Volunteers, particularly those with specialist financial skills, can undertake a number of administrative activities. They can help with:

- Finance, such as bookkeeping and IT.

- Office tasks including reception, stuffing envelopes, database management and input, and so forth.

- Event management.

Guidance
The key roles here that volunteers play are as trustees, directors or other governing roles. Also:

- Mentoring

- Ambassadors

- Advocates

- Experts

- Consultants

- Advisors

Reviewer's Comment
Choosing board members or trustees from volunteers can be very helpful. The staff and management will have good feelings about the individuals and good insight into their personalities. If a person has the will and interest to be an unpaid worker and if he or she works out well in that role, becoming a member of the governing body can be a reward for hard work.

Volunteers want their voluntary work to be well-organised but flexible. The trend toward shorter-term volunteering reflects the demands of modern life on a volunteer's time.

Useful strategies can include:

- Including opportunities for one-off, short-term or drop-in volunteering.

- Having a pool of volunteers to relieve demands on individuals.

- Allowing a flexible rotation system.

Setting Up a Volunteer Programme

Having decided to have a volunteer programme, a number of issues must be considered and addressed.

Senior Management and Trustees

Trustees and senior managers need to understand how volunteers can contribute to the organisation, and they should give volunteers as much attention as they give paid staff. Also, failure to obtain the support of senior staff and trustees can seriously impede or derail a potentially worthwhile volunteer programme.

Volunteering and Diversity

Don't create barriers. Many NPOs fail to attract significant sections of the community, and many groups are underrepresented as volunteers. Be careful not to create a volunteer policy which either discriminates or puts off specific groups from getting involved.

Staffing

Which paid staff member will coordinate volunteer efforts? Will you need to hire someone whose sole role is to look after the volunteers or will you appoint someone already on staff to handle this responsibility part time as part of his or her other responsibilities? Where will the volunteer coordinator fit in the organisation chart? Volunteers need to feel that this leader is directly connected to the NPO's administration or else they will suspect (correctly!) that they have no effective voice.

Resources

What resources will be allocated to support volunteers? Volunteers are not free help. A budget will be necessary to deal with volunteer expenses ranging from printing and postage to transportation reimbursement and insurance. Beyond money, other resources that will be needed are space, IT requirements, training, and staff time for supervision.

Reviewer's Comment

Physical resources can be a significant issue. Volunteers need somewhere to sit and work. They need a desk; most likely, they will need a computer.

It isn't enough to give a volunteer a telephone or a desk that will be needed by staff. There really needs to be a dedicated place for the volunteer and, if at all possible, a place where uncompleted work can be saved until the next time he or she comes in to finish it.

LEGAL REQUIREMENTS

Check how local legislation affects the NPO regarding volunteers. Some areas to look at carefully are:

■ Health and safety legislation. You need to identify what legislation, if any, affects volunteers and take appropriate steps to comply.

■ Insurance coverage. Identify insurance policies your organisation has and whether they can or should be extended to volunteers. Event participation is an area where particular attention is required.

■ Financial safeguards. Any volunteer involved with an organisation's funds should be subject at least to those policies that are in place for paid staff. Other safeguards may be appropriate as well and should be investigated.

PROBLEMS

Consider possible problem areas and how to react if problems occur.

CREATING A VOLUNTEER POLICY

WHY HAVE A POLICY?

A volunteer policy demonstrates commitment to volunteers and helps both staff and volunteers know what is expected. Drawing up a volunteer policy is the ideal time to evaluate and document how volunteers will be involved in your organisation. Don't forget to keep reviewing the policy regularly so that it stays relevant and workable.

WHAT SHOULD BE IN A VOLUNTEER POLICY?

There is no set format for volunteer policies because each NPO has its own needs that should be reflected in its own policy. It is probably best to have a short volunteer policy which refers to other separate documents (covering health and safety, for example). A long document can be very overwhelming. However, there are some areas which should definitely be included:

- A statement of intent. Start the policy with an explanation of what the NPO does and why it involves volunteers in its work. This statement helps clarify intentions both for the organisation writing the policy and for the volunteers reading it.

- Recruitment. Document how the NPO will advertise for, interview and process volunteers. Will references be taken and what checks will be made? How will recruitment materials be made accessible to as many as possible?

- Volunteer roles. Draw up volunteer role outlines or descriptions.

- Induction and training. Include information about how volunteers will be inducted and trained. A trial period is useful and allows volunteers to discover whether they feel comfortable in their role.

- Expenses. Reimbursing volunteers' expenses to the extent possible or desirable means that volunteering is accessible to all, regardless of income. A definitive policy will help avoid misunderstandings later.

- Supervision and support. Delineate what supervision there will be of volunteers.

- Insurance. Include information about insurance coverage to provide comfort to volunteers and those who come in contact with them.

- Legislation. Volunteers may be covered by legislation intended to protect employees as well as by specialised legislation designed for volunteers. Examples of such legislation include equal opportunity laws, discrimination legislation, and health and safety legislation.

- Grievance and disciplinary procedures. Ensure that clear procedures, separate from those for paid staff, are in place to deal with complaints by or about volunteers.

- Confidentiality. Volunteers should be bound by the same requirements for confidentiality as paid staff.

INTRODUCING THE POLICY

It's often useful to introduce the policy with a meeting, which gives a chance to thoroughly explain its importance and answer any questions. All staff, volunteers and prospective volunteers should receive a copy. Display a copy of the policy in prominent places in the building or NPO offices.

READABILITY

Try to make the volunteer policy as accessible as possible. Think about use of language; make it easy to read (for example, use simple language, keeping in mind different abilities or foreign speakers); don't use jargon; and make the print large enough for those with sight problems.

REVISING THE POLICY

The flexible nature of volunteering means that circumstances can change much more quickly than with paid staff, so it makes sense to review the policy at least every year to adapt or improve it.

Current volunteers should be involved because they will have valuable suggestions for improvements, amendments and additions. They will also feel valued by the NPO by being asked to contribute to the policy rather than just working under it.

Written role descriptions or outlines are crucial to creating understanding and clarity both for staff in your organisation and for volunteers. Other benefits include:

- Giving more detailed information to the volunteer about the role than is possible or desirable at the interview.

- Providing a context to show how valuable the activity or task is and how it fits within the work of the organisation.

- Providing a list against which a potential volunteer's skills and expectations can be measured.

- Providing a basis against which to measure the volunteer's performance and activity levels.

- Helping others understand how the volunteer will work with them.

- Offering a reference point when confusion arises or the volunteer stops adhering to the prescribed tasks.

ROLE DESCRIPTIONS

Role descriptions should include the following details:

- Title for the role.

- Objective(s) for the role.

- A broad outline of the tasks and activities to be undertaken.

- Targets or measurements of performance.

They should also include:

- To whom the volunteer reports.

- Location and hours of work.

- Standards of behaviour and dress (if appropriate).

- Skills and qualifications – both the essential and the desirable.

- Necessary personal qualities (if appropriate).

These descriptions might appear to bear close resemblance to job descriptions for paid personnel. This is because they are job descriptions, but for unpaid roles. This attention to detail and effort is desirable as much for the individual volunteer as for each member of staff.

STRUCTURE AND REPORTING

Volunteers find it easier to work within clear boundaries and structures with simple lines of reporting. Supervisory staff should have the appropriate skills and be aware of any special needs that volunteers have. Volunteers need to have confidence in their work and in their understanding of their place in the organisation. It is important that volunteers are given suitable time and attention and good guidance by trained staff.

GROUPS OR COMMITTEES

Sometimes it is valuable for volunteers to work together in groups rather than just individually. Examples are:

- Event committees.

- A group working on the same project.

- Trustees or directors.

- Volunteers at a particular branch or location.

Some groups will be short-term, formed for a particular activity such as a one-time event. Other groups may be ongoing (for example, when volunteers take on events which are done every year).

When seeking to form groups, there are particular issues to deal with. It is sometimes important to prepare a formal plan, especially when the group will have a large degree of independence or will hold sizeable amounts of money on behalf of the NPO.

A formal proposal generally means a written outline as to how the group will operate, and includes details of objectives and goals, the roles and appointment of officers, financial arrangements and controls, and the reporting relationship with the NPO.

Once a group is put together, the same process will occur. This process has been described as follows:

Forming → Storming → Norming → Performing

Forming – getting the group together.

Storming – at this initial stage, personality clashes and differences in approach and expectations can cause conflict, which can either have a beneficial or negative impact. Some groups fail at this stage and fall apart.

Continues on next page

Norming – settling down, the group starts to find its feet and take its first tentative steps.

Performing – an exciting time when momentum builds up and success can turn the group into a powerful force.

If a group is put together artificially by staff members, it may take awhile for the participants to gel because they are more likely to have different roles, mixed objectives, less mutual understanding, and different ways of working. On the other hand, an organically grown group (which starts from a motivated few who then gather a wider group of contacts, colleagues and friends) will have established relationships among its members, which will help them become a team more quickly than a collection of strangers.

Be aware of the dynamics of groups of volunteers in order to ensure they operate appropriately and for the benefit of the volunteers as well as the organisation.

Don't leave groups, however successful, to act in isolation. You need to offer support to maintain performance. Some ways to offer support include:

- Have staff attend key meetings and activities.
- Keep the group up-to-date with developments and news.
- Offer all members of the group the same benefits offered to individual volunteers.
- Keep an eye on group dynamics and act accordingly.
- Celebrate group achievements and anniversaries.
- Maintain contact with all group members, not just officers or leaders of the group.
- Help group members maintain contact with one another and with other volunteers in the organisation.

Groups have a **life span,** so plan ahead for when the group appears to be reaching the end of its life. Success breeds success, so if the group is working well, it is likely that it will attract new members to take over and start the cycle all over again.

RECRUITMENT

Volunteers should be recruited by way of a recruitment drive with sufficient resources put into it. It should be clear what audiences are being targeted. Also, recruitment should be an ongoing process rather than a reaction to an urgent need.

WHAT KINDS OF VOLUNTEERS DOES THE NPO WANT?

When you have established why you want volunteers and what roles volunteers will undertake, you then need to determine what qualities or qualifications the volunteers need to have to undertake those tasks.

Do you want:

- Specific types of volunteers who represent your clients or audience?

- Those with special skills or those willing or able to undertake a variety of roles?

- People with clout in the community?

- Volunteers who will provide diversity of gender, age, race, or other characteristics?

The NPO must decide whom it wants to attract and then plan a recruitment campaign to find these types of volunteers.

METHODS OF RECRUITING VOLUNTEERS

NPOs can get their recruitment messages out through advertising targeted at particular groups, outreach, talks, road shows, presence at public events, websites, word of mouth, asking staff and volunteers for recommendations, and volunteer recruitment organisations.

Ensure that any recruitment messages are clear and easy to understand, and describe the role or roles for which volunteers are being sought. Explain what potential volunteers should do to express their interest in volunteering for your organisation.

Many people who would like to volunteer never do so through lack of information about opportunities.

APPLICATION PROCEDURES

People applying to volunteer prefer procedures that are relaxed and not too bureaucratic. Some may be nervous and

Continues on next page

put off by too many formalities. Provide many ways in which potential volunteers can apply including:

- In person.
- By telephone.
- By email.
- By letter.

Respond to applications quickly with a thank you to all.

SCREENING AND INTERVIEWING

The interview process should reflect the role the volunteer is going to undertake. The larger the role, the more specialised the role, and the longer the job will last all require a more formal, detailed discussion with the prospective person.

Don't fall into the trap of thinking that every person who offers to volunteer or shows interest must be taken on. If there are clear roles and expectations for volunteers, the most appropriate candidates are more likely to be recruited. But careful screening and thoughtful interviewing will expose unsuitable or mismatched candidates early on and avoid embarrassing later attempts to extricate unsuitable volunteers.

REFERENCES

References are useful as another opportunity to identify unsuitable candidates. It is useful to telephone references for information whenever possible (keeping careful record of what was said) because written references can be out-of-date, irrelevant or simply inaccurate. For some roles, criminal record checks or other statutory checks are obligatory, particularly if volunteers will be working with vulnerable clients.

AGREEMENTS AND CONTRACTS

Once someone is taken on as a volunteer, it is important to set some boundaries and ground rules. Ask individuals to sign a statement that covers issues such as:

- Confidentiality.
- Agreement to abide by policies and procedures.
- Rights and responsibilities.
- Expenses and expense reimbursement rules.

SUPPORT AND SUPERVISION

People volunteer for various reasons, but satisfaction with the support and supervision they receive is a key factor in retaining volunteers and encouraging them to volunteer again. Volunteers appreciate personal and professional support and supervision that is not heavy-handed. They also appreciate opportunities for training, socialising with peers and mentoring. They do not appreciate being treated as if they are paid staff. Many volunteers find this off-putting, preferring a balance between efficiency and informality.

INDUCTION

When volunteers start, there should be someone to meet them, introduce them to other volunteers or staff, and show them around. Provide a new volunteer with a welcome packet that contains materials about the organisation, information about the volunteer's role, and contact details for those staff and other volunteers who will and can answer questions. Put it in a format which can be easily updated.

There should be a familiarisation period during which the volunteer has time to understand the work, the work practices, expectations and cultural issues.

TRAINING

Effective training not only equips volunteers with confidence and skills but also reinforces the perception that volunteers are valued.

Training needs vary depending on the role and the volunteer, but training should essentially seek to fill any skills gap between the volunteer and the role he or she is asked to fulfil. Even an experienced volunteer may need help to understand how an NPO approaches and deals with particular tasks.

Offering further training and accreditation options will attract volunteers who are motivated by the desire to improve or learn skills in addition to helping the NPO.

SUPERVISION

It is important that all volunteers clearly understand who their immediate supervisor is as well as any others who are responsible for them.

They will also need to know how supervision will operate (e.g., times and dates of formal appraisal meetings; whether appraisals or discussions about the volunteer's work

Continues on next page

will be in person or by other means; whether such appraisals are formal or informal, or both; whether discussions about work will be in groups or individually).

Volunteers will need to be able to give feedback.

Supervisors themselves need to be monitored and managed carefully to ensure that they are providing effective and appropriate supervision.

CONFLICT RESOLUTION

Conflict is inevitable and can be constructive if handled appropriately, highly destructive if not. The key is to deal with problems as soon as they occur or become obvious. Remember, there should be discipline and grievance procedures set out in your volunteer plan to which both your organisation and the volunteer have agreed. Should conflict occur, be careful to:

■ Identify the problem(s).

■ Get as much information as possible.

■ Listen to all views.

■ Be open and honest.

■ Follow all procedures and policies.

■ Try to reach a resolution.

■ Have an action plan to take the resolution forward.

■ Monitor the situation closely even after resolution is reached.

WHEN VOLUNTEERS GO

No one likes to see volunteers leave. Sometimes they will leave for life changes which are completely unrelated to your organisation, such as moving, taking a new job or having a family. Sometimes they will merely want a new challenge that you are unable to offer, or their role with the NPO will finish. Other times, it will be from dissatisfaction with their role, your organisation or their relationship to it.

Good management practices will limit problems, but the unexpected will happen. Is there the will to "fire" a volunteer if necessary? Is there enough commitment to the value of volunteer involvement that there will not be an overreaction if one volunteer makes a mistake? Have legal liabilities regarding volunteers been clarified, as well as written policies and procedures to protect the organisation, clients and volunteers?

Exit interviews are very useful to gain insight into the volunteer's reasons for leaving and to provide suggestions for improving volunteer policies or rectifying specific problems which had not already been identified.

ENFORCED EXIT

Unsuitable volunteers may get through your recruitment procedures but become unsuitable at a later stage. If the volunteer hasn't worked out, you will still want to maintain a good relationship with him or her.

There are a number of alternatives to asking the volunteer to leave. These might include:

- Offering a new role.

- Modifying the current role.

- Providing additional training.

- Revising supervision practices with respect to that volunteer.

- Changing the volunteer's supervisor or group.

If these ideas are not practical or don't work, consider referring the volunteer to a more appropriate organisation.

If none of these suggestions resolve the problem or are appropriate, find a way to say goodbye to the volunteer as positively as possible.

Show appreciation to your volunteers regularly, fairly, appropriately and sincerely! It is good policy and practice to do so. Disillusioned or dissatisfied volunteers make disastrous ambassadors for an organisation.

Every situation is different. Cultural issues in different places must be considered when determining ways of thanking or recognising volunteers. Notice what other NPOs with successful volunteer programmes are doing, talk to colleagues, and ask your own volunteers for input.

Volunteers are not working for a salary and therefore need a different type of recognition than paid staff. At the very least, volunteers will want to feel welcomed, respected, informed, needed, effectively used and managed. But they may also want or expect more.

Some ideas for ways in which NPOs can recognise or reward volunteers include:

- Give practical help and advice on subjects of interest.

- Continue to provide training – always a way of reinvigorating interest and enthusiasm.

- Publicise volunteers and their achievements and contributions in annual reports, publications and newsletters; on websites; and at meetings.

- Trustees and senior management should thank volunteers to show that their work is appreciated at the very top of the organisation.

- Give volunteers opportunities to socialise with their peers and staff.

- Ask for ideas, opinions and feedback.

- Offer extra responsibility or forms of promotion.

- Give volunteer awards and honours.

- Show interest in them as individuals.

- Recognise that for some volunteers, leaving the organisation to attain further goals is also an achievement or success.

Reviewer's Comment

Heartfelt appreciation can mean everything to the volunteer, even more than all the formal appreciation policies devised by an organisation. An informal party to thank a helper is priceless and can only be done if staff members really appreciate what the volunteer is doing. It doesn't work in some environments, but when it does, it is magic.

My advice would be to say "thank you! thank you! thank you!" all of the time – every time the volunteer comes into the office, after every email, in every note and letter. Everyone on the staff should thank the volunteer for each visit. It never gets old, and the volunteer wants to come back because he or she is so visibly appreciated.

Measuring Impact and Evaluating Contribution

Many NPOs use a method or formula to value the contribution of their volunteers in terms of time and money.

Valuing the contribution made by volunteers in terms of money may be relatively straightforward. You can multiply the hours that volunteers give to the organisation by a set hourly rate for each job. Remember to also assign a value for staff time spent working with volunteers in order to obtain a true picture of the volunteers' worth to the NPO.

Valuing the contribution made by volunteers in terms of good will raised for the organisation is much more difficult to value, and a subjective analysis based on anecdote, interviews and discussions will be required.

Schedule regular status reviews to assess whether and how the volunteer programme is changing over time.

■ Are the original goals and objectives for the volunteer programme still relevant?

■ Is it necessary to add more paid coordinating staff?

■ How large should the volunteer programme become?

■ What are the problems?

■ What are the successes?

Involving both staff and volunteers in the analysis and reporting process will give both sides confidence that they are valued and that the programme is valued and important to the organisation.

Final Thoughts

No matter what volunteers do, the common denominator is that there is always competition for good volunteers!

The challenge for many NPOs is to get the best people and make the best use of them.

Those organisations that make a serious commitment to their volunteers and work hard to support them are most likely to be successful.

AUTHOR

CHERRY BUSHELL

Cherry Bushell has extensive experience in all aspects of charity and nonprofit work, both on the administration side and the fundraising side. She worked with one of the UK's largest charities, Macmillan Cancer Relief, where she managed a variety of fundraising mechanisms with national, small and medium-sized companies, as well as trusts, foundations and individual donors. She directed promotional and special events, and ran a community programme which involved coordinating committee networks, retail outlets, youth and school groups, and local volunteer associations.

In her work with smaller charities, Cherry raised funds by means of corporate partnerships, social and sporting events, trusts, major donors, auctions and celebrity endorsements. In particular, she was responsible for liaising with celebrities, the royal patron and other high-profile supporters.

Interacting with staff, volunteers and the general community has been an ongoing part of Cherry's career.

Cherry has a BA (Hons) degree in Modern History, Economic History and Politics.

Jinny Gender, Reviewer

Jinny Gender has a degree in Sociology from Lindenwood College in St. Charles, Missouri. In a nonprofit career spanning 30 years, Jinny has served on dozens of nonprofit boards – as president of many – and has worked tirelessly as a volunteer. The late Missouri Governor Mel Carnahan appointed her to the Missouri Board of Social Workers in 1994 where she was the first public member ever.

In the last 10 years alone, Jinny has served on 20 nonprofit boards including: National Public Radio KWMU in St. Louis, past president; Metro St. Louis Women's Political Caucus, past president; ALIVE, Alternatives to Living in Violent Environments, past president; Lindenwood Alumni Club, past president; Charter board member of the St. Louis County Shelter for Abused Women; Confluence, St. Louis; Magic House, Museum for Children; and Y.E.S., Youth Emergency Service. She has been a hearing tester for the Special School district for 20 years and has had her own weekly talk-radio show on station WGNU in St. Louis for the last 10 years. With a partner, Jinny Gender has her own consulting business, International Charity Consultants.

*Quick*GUIDES

everything you need to know...fast

MOTIVATING STAFF

by Lorraine Romeril-Smith

reviewed by Debbie Holmes

WIREMILL
PUBLISHING LTD

Across the world the organizations and institutions that fundraise to finance their work are referred to in many different ways. They are charities, non-profits or not-for-profit organizations, non-governmental organizations (NGOs), voluntary organizations, academic institutions, agencies, etc. For ease of reading, we have used the term Nonprofit Organization, Organization or NPO as an umbrella term throughout the *Quick*Guide series. We have also used the spellings and punctuation used by the author.

Published by
Wiremill Publishing Ltd.
Edenbridge, Kent TN8 5PS, UK
info@wiremillpublishing.com
www.wiremillpublishing.com
www.quickguidesonline.com

British Library Cataloguing in Publication Data
A catalogue record for this book is available from the British Library.

ISBN Number 1-905053-21-5

Printed by Rhythm Consolidated Berhad, Malaysia
Cover Design by Jennie de Lima and Edward Way
Design by Colin Woodman Design

CONTENTS

MOTIVATING STAFF

Introduction

Motivation is all about connecting with the people who report to you so they feel inspired to meet the challenges that your organisation faces. As a manager or supervisor, you know that you are supposed to be motivating your staff. You also know that it is just one of the many tasks you need to fit into the average day. With so many demands on your time, it isn't surprising that sometimes the motivation gets left behind. The good news is that you cannot make anyone do something that he or she doesn't want to do. This *Quick*Guide will make it clear that all motivation is self-motivation. So don't beat yourself up over the fact that your staff's motivation may be missing a few beats! The better news is that as a leader, you can influence and cajole your people into becoming self-motivated.

There have been many experts who have spent a lot of time studying what motivates people. Throughout this *Quick*Guide, you will find practical guidelines to help you motivate the people for whom you are responsible. It is your skill as a manager to practice what you preach that makes the biggest difference. The practical ideas contained in this Guide will help you identify what you are doing right. You will also be able to identify what you can add to your management skills to make a positive difference. Recognising your role in helping your people become self-motivated is one of the keys to success in any type of organisation.

What Is Motivation?

Are you clear on what motivation really is? Let's take a look at the definitions.

Motivation is anything that causes somebody to do something in response. There are lots of words that can be swapped with "motivating." Motivating is about prompting, activating, moving, inspiring, inciting, inducing, stimulating, provoking, influencing, encouraging, causing, exciting, urging, goading, rousing, arousing, stirring, wheedling, coaxing, persuading, cajoling, tempting, pushing, driving, or instigating people to do things. Motivating can be done verbally, physically or psychologically. With all of these words to choose from, you may find that you are actually motivating people around you a lot more than you realise!

Reading up on some of the motivational theories can assist you in understanding people's needs. Once you have an understanding of people's needs, you can use that information to help improve a worker's performance. Regardless of how many guru tips you pick up, be mindful of the overriding factor that once a need has been met, it no longer has the power to motivate!

There are patterns to what motivates people. Understanding the patterns can help you identify what kind of group or person you are working with. Some people or group patterns fall into the following categories:

- Self-motivated person (Remember that all motivation comes from within.)
- Work team (voluntary or paid)
- Project team
- Business strategy team
- Task force
- Customer service team
- Sales team
- Maintenance team
- Veteran, baby boomer, generation X, generation Y
- Dependent or independent

Continues on next page

What Is Motivation?

Some managers and supervisors make the mistake of thinking that what motivates them also motivates their employees. Take a moment to think about what motivates you.

- What factors are important to you in your working life?
- What has motivated you in the past?
- What has de-motivated you in the past?
- What motivates you in the short term?
- What motivates you in the long term?

Find out what things motivate each person on your team. Some of the things that influence different people to perform well in their jobs include:

- Money
- Being paid above market rate
- Respect
- Achievement
- Being able to make a difference
- Responsibility
- Growth
- Having set processes
- An attractive work environment
- A challenging work environment
- A creative environment
- Praise
- Additional leave
- Feeling like part of the team
- Wearing a uniform
- Not having to wear a uniform
- Wearing casual clothing to work
- Getting dressed up for work
- Contributing ideas
- Travel
- Not having to travel
- Training
- Short study courses
- Conferences, seminars and retreats
- Promotions
- Camaraderie
- Recognition

What Is Motivation?

- Awards
- Telecommuting
- Flexible work schedules
- Free parking
- Flexible benefits
- Independence
- Bonuses
- Being appreciated
- Believing in the philosophy and vision
- Having pride in what they do
- Working with other people
- Cultural diversity
- Being able to trust colleagues

Recognise that people are motivated by their own individual goals, values and desires. Find out what really motivates your people by asking them.

Ask them what they want most from their jobs and listen really well to what they say.

Ask them:

- In casual conversations
- Using open-ended questions
- In surveys
- In individual or team meetings
- In performance appraisals

You would think that you have the magic formula once you have learned what kind of need motivates somebody to work. Wrong! People have different needs at different times in their lives depending on their age, health, and personal and family circumstances. We must continue to be aware of what motivates each individual.

BENEFITS OF MOTIVATING YOUR STAFF

High staff motivation provides visible and hidden benefits to any type of organisation. Employees who love their jobs and their workplace typically:

- Contribute more actively to the business.
- Achieve more goals.
- Manage their own development.
- Help others with their development.
- Display self-esteem.
- Are highly capable.
- Get more done and have more ideas.
- Focus on the positive.
- Support the organisational culture.
- Treat clients and co-workers with more respect.
- Serve as ambassadors for the organisation.

A highly motivated workforce can have a huge impact on the productivity of your organisation because it:

- Increases staff morale.
- Increases job satisfaction.
- Generates a harmonious workplace.
- Increases loyalty.
- Encourages employees to promote the organisation.
- Increases productivity.
- Reduces staff turnover and its associated costs.

Creating and then maintaining a motivated workforce requires strong leadership and commitment. If you want your people to meet organisational objectives, then you must set high standards and give employees something to get excited about. Employees expect to be managed by someone who is trustworthy, who cares about them as well as the organisation, and who acts with integrity. There is no substitute for effective day-to-day leadership when it comes to creating and maintaining a motivated workforce.

Tips for being an effective leader:

- Be aware that your arrival at work sets the tone for the day.
- Lead by example and get involved.
- Work with employees as colleagues.
- Believe that people are your only resource.
- Manage your time so that you can focus on doing the right thing.
- Spend 20 percent of your time doing the one thing that will achieve overall objectives.
- Hire the right people with the right attitude.
- Induct and train your people.
- Negotiate achievable goals.
- Define the standards.
- Measure the outcomes.
- Share the results.
- Appraise the individuals.
- Create and communicate an honest vision for your organisation.
- Encourage employees to do things they never considered doing.
- Listen actively to what your employees have to say and take action.
- Be consistent in everything you do.
- Keep everyone informed about what's happening in the organisation.
- Provide opportunities to socialise.
- Practice personal integrity and fairness.
- Provide frequent feedback that reinforces what people do well.

Continues on next page

How to Be a Motivating Leader

- Use simple, powerful, motivational words.

- Provide work that stimulates growth.

- Find out what your employees are really good at doing.

- Ask your employees what they like to do.

- Provide the right rewards and incentives to reinforce the standards.

- Use recognition to reinforce the standards.

- Create an environment in which people practice self-reliance.

- Deal with employees who are not pulling their weight.

- Delegate the right tasks to the right people.

- Match people's abilities to the job.

- Be able to recognise weaknesses and strengths in yourself.

- Find and use the right resources.

- Provide opportunities for professional development.

- Help your employees feel good about the work they do.

- Build teamwork.

- Remove de-motivators.

- Demonstrate support.

- Be alert for signs of burnout.

- Believe that people want to do the best they can.

MEASURING MORALE

You can't force your people to have good morale. You can't order it or buy it. Morale is highly contagious, and everyone is affected by it. It is important to be able to measure the morale of your workforce. Morale grows over a long period of time out of good human relations. As a manager or leader, your human relations skills are vital. Morale grows out of respect for the individual, recognition of individual differences, good communication, understanding and counselling.

It is important to measure the staff morale because it:

■ Gives people a chance to say what is on their mind.

■ Tells management what the workers are thinking.

■ Indicates to people that you care.

■ Focuses your attention on morale.

■ Usually equals greater quality and output.

■ Encourages greater cooperation.

To show an improvement in morale, you need a way to measure where you are now and set goals for where you want to be. You will know how much you have achieved when you measure morale and compare it to the initial measurement.

■ Some organisations run a staff satisfaction survey. Results are summarised, graphed and presented back to the team.

■ To obtain examples of surveys that could be adapted for your use, search on the Internet using the phrase "staff satisfaction survey."

■ Some managers and supervisors can "feel" where their team is on a scale of one to ten.

■ Some managers count the number of staff members smiling each day in order to give themselves a percentage factor.

Find a way that works for you.

Signs of low morale include:

■ High turnover of staff

■ No respect for managers or supervisors

■ Low productivity

■ Excessive waste

■ High number of grievances

Continues on next page

- General lack of cooperation
- Poor-quality work
- Excessive sick leave
- Excessive lateness and absenteeism
- Poor timekeeping
- Longer lunch periods
- Loss of interest and enthusiasm
- No role models or leaders
- No performance measurement
- No pride in the work

What can you do to build morale?

- Give your people worthwhile goals on which to focus.
- Ensure objectives are clear and manageable.
- Make sure people are clear about their roles.
- Create a climate in which morale can develop.
- Create a fun working environment.
- Look after the general working conditions.
- Criticise privately and constructively.
- Be sure pay is fair and equitable.
- Talk with everyone regarding performance and progress.
- Help people succeed.
- See how you can add interest, challenge and variety.
- Demonstrate the importance of commitment.
- Be truthful in all your actions.
- Reinforce job security.
- Make the work interesting.
- Express appreciation.
- Communicate openly.
- Encourage and acknowledge employees' ideas.
- Show consideration for their feelings.
- Assign new people to the appropriate team.
- Be people-centred in your management.
- Match people's needs with the organisation's needs.

- Try to assign jobs that satisfy employees.
- Make sure people get rewards they value.
- Remember that motivation comes from within.
- Help people achieve their personal goals.
- Create clear standards and objectives.
- Provide adequate job training.
- Offer supportive supervision.
- Allow opportunities for advancement.
- Treat each person as an individual.
- Be the role model for your people.
- Promote participation in decision making.
- Promote cooperation and teamwork.
- Make sure staff members know they belong.
- Seek and give feedback.
- Be sincere with praise when it is justified.
- Resolve conflict.

THINGS YOU HAVE NO CONTROL OVER

You have no control over family relationships or whom your people associate with away from work. Yet these factors can affect a person's attitude dramatically! Be alert to these factors and their existence, and do what you can to reduce their impact.

Reviewer's Comment

The ideas here are great, and it's good for managers to be reminded of all these things. It's useful to think of these items under headings of Objectives, Management, Pastoral Care (or Team Building), and Personal Behaviour. For example, feedback could be in the Objectives section, whereas people-centred management could be in Personal Behaviour. By categorising these ideas, you can decide which items are more significant within the context of your organisation or which items are more useful given different types of staff.

People like to know what is going on in their workplace. There are many ways that you can keep your staff informed. Listed below are some ways that are used effectively. Identify the ones that you are already using and those which you would like to try. The more ways that you use to communicate, the stronger the message will be.

MEETINGS

There are a lot of meetings held that waste a lot of people's time. Well-planned meetings are an effective communication tool. Consider a regular meeting time with your team. Ensure that for each meeting:

- There is an objective to the meeting.

- You have invited input on the agenda items (which eliminates surprises).

- You have sent out an agenda in advance.

- Each agenda item has a time limit (and the person leading that agenda item is advised of it).

- Only people who need to be there have been invited.

- The room and equipment are set up.

- You have found a visual way to illustrate or demonstrate your key message.

- You arrive early and start on time.

- Half of the meeting time includes training.

- The action points are noted and distributed immediately after the meeting.

STAND-UP MEETINGS

When you need to get a message out fast to your workforce, try calling a stand-up meeting. No chairs are involved, which implies that the meeting will be short!

FACE-TO-FACE MEETINGS

Meet regularly with your people one-on-one. People want to know that they are being listened to, and they look for feedback. Meeting individually and privately for ten minutes a week provides an ideal opportunity to discuss the numbers, targets and issues that have been mutually identified as focus points.

COMMUNICATING WITH YOUR STAFF

INFORMAL FACE-TO-FACE DISCUSSIONS

If you have something to say to someone, the first choice of communication is face-to-face. Don't email or telephone if it is very simple to talk directly with your people as you walk the job.

TELEPHONES

■ Sometimes the fastest way to deal with a letter, email or other incoming communication is by telephone.

■ Regular teleconferences are easy to set up with two or more people and can become another opportunity to listen, and to provide leadership and feedback. Teleconferences are particularly effective when your people are geographically spread out (making face-to-face meetings too expensive or time-consuming).

■ Mobile phones are an essential business tool for your people when they are out and about. They assist in providing an instant link with what is going on at the office, and they enable co-workers to keep field staff informed.

■ Consider SMS messaging when you want to get an important message to all of your team members.

■ Consider phones for your team members that can be easily coordinated and updated with their computers, diaries and other communication tools.

COMPUTERS

Technology is always advancing. Learn about and embrace any new opportunities to use technology to communicate to your people in the way they want to be communicated with.

■ Provide training so that your team knows how to store and retrieve information from your network.

■ Provide all the information that people need to know in order to access your network or intranet site.

■ Sometimes use emails in place of memos.

■ Write a great headline in the email's "subject" field to ensure your message gets through the clutter.

Continues on next page

COMMUNICATING WITH YOUR STAFF

- Provide training to your team on how to manage their email program.

- Know how to secure and track important or confidential emails.

- Teach your team how to schedule appointments and meetings through their electronic diaries.

- Consider the ability to view your team's electronic diaries and consider allowing your team to view yours.

- Ensure your team members have the right computers and technology tools to communicate effectively.

NEWSLETTERS

- Newsletters provide information to staff on what is going on in the workplace.

- They are excellent tools for providing positive feedback and recognition.

- Distributing newsletters regularly is more important than production quality.

- They can be printed, copied or emailed.

- Newsletters should have a structure of regular sections and articles.

- Good editing ensures that the messages going out are in line with the vision and current objectives.

PERSONAL AND TARGETED COMMUNICATION

- Use handwritten cards or notes for birthdays, achievements, recognition, and thank-you notes. Staff may delete an email but may keep or remember something you wrote by hand!

- Whiteboards and blackboards can be used for messages or information that you need to have right in front of your people as they work.

- Use boards to put up notices in areas where staff members take their breaks.

- A communication sign-in book is handy when you have staff coming and going on various shifts and at various times. Important messages go into the book, and staff sign that they have read the information.

COMMUNICATING WITH YOUR STAFF

■ The office refrigerator makes a creative whiteboard.

■ Share industry information that comes in the way of magazines, journals, articles or reports of importance. On the front of each copy, staple a pre-printed note that reads "For your information. Please read and pass on." List the names of all team members and provide an area for the "time" that the copy was sent on. Using the word "time" rather than "day" creates a sense of urgency.

■ Build a library of resource materials about your industry. Include personal-development material. Make it available to everyone.

■ Encourage your team to use the CDs and tapes in their cars.

USE POWERFUL WORDS
Words are powerful tools that we can use to motivate. Using simple, powerful words like "please" and "thank you" can make someone's day. How many powerful words and phrases do you currently have in your tool kit?

■ Use sentences beginning with "what," "where," "when," "why," "how" and "who" to help you open up discussions or meetings.

■ Use words such as "would," "could" and "should" to help you get an answer or agreement.

■ Use "you" or "yours" when writing anything.

■ Use manners by saying "please," "thank you," "you're welcome."

■ Notice and tell people when they have done something good.

■ When people have done something wrong, always tell them privately. Use the PCP formula: Praise, Criticise and Praise.

The first step in creating a motivational work environment is to stop taking actions that de-motivate people. Identify and take the actions that will motivate your workforce. The design of your work environment can influence how well your people thrive. Find out how to clear the fog and make the workplace enjoyable with the resources you have.

BUILD TRUST

You have nothing without the trust of your staff. When trust is present, everything else is easier.

RULES AND POLICIES

People flourish in a workplace where all employees live by the same rules. If you create an environment that is viewed as fair and consistent, you give people less to complain about.

- The fewer rules you have, the better.

- Keep policies only if they protect your organisation legally or create order.

- Publish the rules and policies.

- Educate all employees to ensure they are aware of the policies.

- Identify organisational values with your workers.

- Include any professional codes of conduct in the education process.

EMPLOYEE INVOLVEMENT

Employee involvement requires that people be competent to make decisions about their work.

- Let your people know that they are expected to make decisions that will improve their work.

- Reward and recognise the people who make decisions that improve their work.

- Share your organisation's mission and values so team members can focus their involvement appropriately.

- When employees come to you, ask them what they think they should do.

- Intervene as a coach when you know that a problem is looming.

- If you have already decided what you will do in a particular situation, don't ask for ideas.

- Almost any decision is improved with input.

CREATING THE RIGHT ENVIRONMENT

- People who have high self-esteem are more likely to improve the work environment.

- Provide the opportunity for people to fully develop their abilities.

- Find out what people want and give it to them.

UNDERSTANDING MAINTENANCE FACTORS

Clean bathrooms may not motivate good performance; however, if they're not clean, people will complain about them. Therefore, cleaning the bathroom becomes a maintenance factor. Ensure that maintenance factors are taken care of.

DESIGN AN INTERESTING WORK SPACE

Some questions for you to ask:

- Is the workplace you provide comfortable, clean and well-maintained?

- Is the place aesthetically pleasing to the eye?

- Are employees able to make cleaning recommendations that are acted upon?

- Is the lighting good enough for all tasks and in all areas?

- Have you allowed your people to personalise their work space?

- Are there pictures on the walls that people like?

- Have you addressed the parking issues fairly?

- Is there enough space per person?

- Is there a lunchroom where your people can get away from the work?

- Are staff members aware of your concern for their health and safety?

- Is your office furniture in good repair and appropriate for the tasks?

- Do you have regular fire drills?

- Do your people know what to do in emergency situations?

- Is all electrical equipment checked professionally and on a regular schedule?

- Do all staff members have the right equipment to do their jobs?

- Is there a place where people can work privately when they need to?

- Do you allow flexitime so that people can come in early or stay late to get work done?

Continues on next page

■ Do you allow people to work at home when they have to meet a tough deadline?

GET YOUR PEOPLE OUT OF THE OFFICE

For staff members who are stuck in the traditional office, there are benefits in getting them out. It's a bit like sending them on holiday for a change of scenery. Some options:

■ Hold some of your meetings off-site.

■ For those who never get out of the office, a work-related trip could make a difference in their morale.

■ The gift that is greatest of all, to many people, is the gift of time. Send them home to do what they want to do when you are looking for a suitable reward.

■ Job sharing is another flexibility option that you can add to your motivational tool belt.

■ Consider providing sabbaticals in a time frame that works for your organisational structure.

Reviewer's Comment
Sometimes it is impossible for an individual manager to influence many items on these lists. Some will be a central HR or office management function. For example, allowing people to work at home may be within an individual's control while creating a lunchroom or parking facility may not be.

Each organisation will be different, and the reader should determine which things he or she can realistically do and which things he or she can refer to others in the organisation.

HIRING, INDUCTING AND TRAINING

You hire people because they have qualifications and experience that interest you. But nobody comes equipped with all that is needed to work at your specific organisation.

HIRE RIGHT
If you hire right, you can save yourself a lot of grief.

- Always be on the lookout for people who would be ideal for your workplace.
- Work with your HR department or recruitment consultancy if you have one.
- Ensure the job description has been updated.
- Advertise the position using an attention-getting headline.
- Check references.
- Put a warm, welcome tone into your letter of appointment.

INDUCT RIGHT
On the first day:

- Treat your new people like royalty.
- Make sure everyone knows that they are arriving and how to welcome them.

- Give them your induction materials to introduce guidelines and advice.
- Arrange for the recruit to have morning tea or coffee and lunch with new colleagues.
- Get them on the phone list, set up their email, and have printed business cards ready.

During the first quarter:

- Show them the work.
- Agree on goals, standards and time frames.
- Commence regular one-on-one meetings.
- Find out what the person already knows.
- Agree on the training schedule.
- Review the results.

PROFESSIONAL DEVELOPMENT
Invest time and money in your people's ongoing professional development. Budget for each employee to attend at least one networking function, conference or workshop each year. Make sure the event isn't something they are forced to attend, like compulsory training, and is something they have a role in choosing.

One important criterion in employee selection is picking the best person you can find for the job. Another is establishing clear goals with measures so the individual can succeed. Without measurement, without challenge, how does the person or team measure its success or get organised?

SET CLEAR AND MEASURABLE GOALS

Day-to-day management is about tracking information and data about staff; it's not about controlling the people. Work with your people to collect information about their performance in simple, fast and meaningful ways.

- Know what the key organisational objectives are.

- Set all individual and group activity goals in relation to the objectives.

- Set activities that can be measured in numbers or outcomes.

- Set targets by service, key constituents, and budgets.

- Break activity goals into weekly numbers.

- Discuss the results and focus ahead with each person and with the entire team.

MEASURING FOR SUCCESS

Measuring for success is about motivating, guiding and directing employees to achieve their targets and give their best.

- Performance management is a key tool in employee motivation.

- Performance assessment is a tool for improving staff motivation and satisfaction.

- Giving positive feedback and rewarding performance can be great motivators.

- Give positive feedback on a regular basis.

- A performance review has become a staple of business management.

- Typically given once or twice a year, the performance review incorporates both positive feedback and constructive criticism.

Rewards and Recognition

Reward Excellence

When an employee does great things, do something to reward the success.

Be mindful that intrinsic motivation is much stronger than extrinsic motivation. Personal interests and challenges are often much stronger than outside motivators such as money. Some ways to reward good performance:

- Thank them!
- Give a promotion.
- Increase salary.
- Provide a bonus.

- Upgrade a title.
- Increase responsibility.
- Tie performance to pay.

Recognition

- Give recognition for individual performance.
- Share the success in the newsletter and in meetings.
- Ask them what they want.
- Provide a gift.
- Write a thank-you note.

Final Thoughts

Reviewer's Comment

Managers need to manage staff expectations more than anything else. They need to determine which elements motivate and which of those elements are deliverable. In my experience, staff may want a certain type of training, but it could simply be far too expensive for a nonprofit organisation that is operating on a limited budget.

Managers should be reassured that they don't have to, and probably can't, meet every developmental and motivational need of their employees.

AUTHOR

LORRAINE ROMERIL-SMITH

Lorraine Romeril-Smith is one of Australia's most respected advertising and media professionals. Having held senior management roles with newspapers in New Zealand and Australia, Vogue Magazines and advertising agencies, Lorraine has developed an unparalleled understanding of all facets of working with and motivating a wide variety of teams.

As General Manager for hma Blaze Advertising Agency's Queensland operation, Lorraine manages a team working with local, state and nationally based accounts. These accounts cover a wide range of industry sectors including recruitment, health care, education, tourism and local government. In addition to these commercial clients, Lorraine has overall responsibility for the management and direction of the Queensland-based activities of the agency's Commonwealth Government account.

Lorraine is recognised by the media as a knowledgeable source on advertising and management issues. She is often invited to speak at conferences, functions and events. Lorraine lectures at the Queensland University of Technology in advertising and provides training in the fields of advertising and sales management through her company, Romeril-Smith Media Advertising and Training. She was a finalist in the 2004 Telstra Queensland Business Woman of the Year.

Debbie Holmes, Reviewer

Debbie Holmes is the Director of Fundraising at Terrence Higgins Trust, the UK's leading HIV and AIDS charity where she is responsible for a voluntary income target of £4 million. She has worked as a fundraiser and fundraising manager in the UK voluntary (charitable) sector since 1990. She currently manages a staff of 16 and has recently developed and implemented a three-year strategy to support the growth of voluntary income.